Boy, Mother
Caroline Bracken

smith|doorstop

the poetry business

Published 2025 by
Smith|Doorstop Books
The Poetry Business
Campo House,
54 Campo Lane,
Sheffield S1 2EG

Copyright © Caroline Bracken
All Rights Reserved

ISBN 978-1-914914-91-1
Typeset by Utter
Printed by People for Print, Sheffield

Smith|Doorstop Books are a member of Inpress:
www.inpressbooks.co.uk

Distributed by NBN International, 1 Deltic Avenue,
Rooksley, Milton Keynes MK13 8LD

The Poetry Business gratefully acknowledges the support of Arts Council England.

Contents

5	Amor Matris
6	Hyperemesis Gravidarum
8	Uninvited Guest
10	Admissions
12	The Wayfarer
14	Events
15	Cé Leis Thú? (Who Do You Belong To?)
16	Word Salad
17	Ward Warning
18	Mental Health Act
20	Eyewitness
22	The One Where You Look at an Ancient Painting and See Your Son
23	Fabric
24	On the Occasion of Learning That He is Missing
26	Ballast
27	Black Coat
28	The Blues
29	Coffee Sonnet
30	Marks and Sparks
32	Legacy
34	Acknowledgements

for Michelle, Conor and Ian

Amor Matris

Some
children
are easy
to raise, they eat
tidy orange segments, wipe their fingers,
sleep, spring on balanced feet towards known goals.
Others startle
at changes
in light,
sound.

Some
mothers
are easy
to love, they wear
fuchsia lipstick, carry designer bags,
take up wild swimming or mountaineering.
Others struggle
to go out
their front
door.

Hyperemesis Gravidarum

In the Pacific a killer whale bites a chinook salmon
feeds half to her son
she will do this until one of them dies
her devotion means the chance of her belly swelling
with another baby orca
is reduced by fifty per cent.

Her older daughter must find her own fish.

I was fed by a drip for the first trimester
of my son's life. My daughter was five
she learned early that mothers sometimes
can't be relied on.

I lay on that hospital bed and prayed
for him to be born in one piece
but starvation does damage
he will need me until one of us dies.

My belly never swelled again.

Today the Irish Sea is quiet
the East and West piers curve towards each other
arms that cannot meet
the space between them a channel
for a flotilla of blue and white yachtlets
sailing into harbour.

The stocks of chinook salmon are endangered
there are only seventy-three killer whales left
and I'm not saying humans are the same
but there's something about a boy's hunger
that breaks a mother in two

makes her sacrifice the thought of future children
on the altar of her living daughter
for the sake of one pale desperate son.

Uninvited Guest

Two months
after your eighteenth birthday
Psychiatry moved
into our boxroom.

Reeking of bleach
he was clean at least
well-read   fond
of polysyllabic words
convoluted sentences   footnotes.

Wrecked my head with case-studies
stacked peer-reviewed journals
like Jenga
behind the door.

Decided he didn't care
for the view
of our back yard
bins were not his thing
insisted on inhabiting the front

bedroom – mine. I resisted
but there was no talking to him
so for peace I gave in. He invaded
the kitchen   claimed the living room.

His DSM[1] fetish
was embarrassing
I stopped inviting visitors
locked him in the shed for a week

but he climbed out the window
crawled into the conservatory
through the cat-flap –
he got worse after that.

I sent the dog to kennels
resigned from my job
sold the car. The only
place safe from his gaze
was your room.

It must have been
the sounds put him off –
not a rap fan apparently
or maybe it was the grey
ashtrays unchanged

sheets   empty pizza boxes
24/7 gaming   wolf howling.
Whatever it was
he never crossed your threshold.

He issued me with an ultimatum –
it was you or him.
He won. The house breathes now

I sleep easy most nights
but sometimes
I wake early
miss your music
hear him snoring.

---

[1] Psychiatry never explains himself.

Admissions

i

The waiting room outside the admissions office is like any other
bloated blue chairs with foam poking through torn corners
the handiwork of some previous impatient patient
greasy Hello magazines show Princess Diana alive
accepting a pink posy from an overdressed child
a half-full water cooler   no cups.

ii

You tick boxes   hope he won't notice the locked door
too late   he yanks the handle   bangs on the high window
screams and spits words which bounce off you like sponge-balls
three of them take him through another locked door
you are released   you sit in your car smoke a cigarette
phone your sister   hang up   you do not cry.

iii

Press the buzzer   the door opens   press the next buzzer
longer this time   you are interrupting their form-filling
they search your bag like airport security   you wish you were
boarding a plane to somewhere   anywhere
his right hand is bloody and bruised from punching walls
you ask questions   no answers   he is eighteen
they can't engage with you.

iv

You tell a few people   they suggest acupuncture   aromatherapy   yoga
you stop telling people   he gains ten pounds   you lose ten
you can afford them   other relatives tell their stories in the smoking shelter
everybody smokes   the stories are all the same   some are on their tenth

admission   they say there is no cure   no hope   only endurance
only acceptance   only helplessness   you stop talking to them
you refuse to stop asking questions   you take him home.

v

He refuses all meds   you are poisoning him   there is an incident
you call the police   they take him away   he goes quietly
talking about football   another admission   and another   and another
and another until you lose count   he is an adult   make his own choices
he wanders the streets   you make calls   lobby politicians   argue with doctors
you will not give up   they give in   find him a safe place   he is stable
you can rest   for now.

The Wayfarer
after 'The Wayfarer' painting by Jheronimus Bosch c.1500

It's a struggle to leave behind
brown ochre, umber, grey, bone black.
Arms restricted by the strap
attached to a basket on his back
every step on one boot
one slipper hurts his bloodied calf.

A print of the painting hangs in the foyer of the psychiatric facility.

He carries the cobbler's tools
his grandfather gifted him
an awl and yarn
stuck in his hat for safekeeping
a knife by his side
for just in case.

A notice says No Phones. No Shoelaces. No Belts. No Weapons.

A shillelagh protects him
from rabid dogs and vagabonds
his cheekbones are sunken from hunger
but he knows his grandfather survived
the plague and remembers his words
Press on son, push through.

The people here speak in tongues. Some of them are not real.

He throws one last look
over his shoulder at pigs feeding
his feet face the wooden gate
where a fatted calf waits
and there may be a touch
of lead-tin yellow, an infusion of blue.

Colour is a construct of eye and brain. It does not exist in objects.

Events

Two Malaysian Airlines planes fell from the sky
Germany beat Argentina in the World Cup final
President Higgins went to Windsor Castle to meet the Queen
Happy by Pharrell Williams spent ten weeks at number one
The Rosie Hackett Bridge over the River Liffey opened
President Obama went to Cuba to meet Raul Castro
The Tuam babies horror went international
Garth Brookes had his Croke Park gigs cancelled
President Higgins went to China to meet Xi Jinping
One hundred thousand people marched against water charges
Shutthefrontdoor won the Irish Grand National
President Obama went to Vatican City to meet the Pope
Scotland voted against independence
Russia annexed Crimea
I don't remember any of these events
I remember an eleven-hour wait in A&E you drifting further
and further away from me the doctor saying they had no bed
for you there we weren't in the catchment area me thanking God
for health insurance the private hospital registrar's reassurance
that it wouldn't be for too long I didn't know he was wrong
I remember wondering if you had taken something like teenagers do
but it was nothing you had done something had taken you son.

Cé Leis Thú? (Who Do You Belong To?)

my son is a Ming vase I carried him under my skin for 293 days safe in an amniotic fluid caul he was born fragile I minded him as best I could wore white gloves while bathing him in milk shielded his cobalt blue eyes from the sun kept him hydrated fed him ghost orchids fire lilies and black bat flowers placed him at my bedside every night told him fantastical tales about dragons and dinosaurs polished him free of dust with a lambskin chamois closed the blinds to protect his ceramic body from fading you know what's coming so I won't say it and there'll be none of that crap about cracks are where the light gets in no shade on leonard cohen or kintsugi I run my fingers over my son's wounds break my skin on their uneven edges catch the blood in my mouth before it drips tell him it's nothing no more than a paper cut I wrap him in a cashmere blanket sit him in the passenger seat remind him to buckle up we're going off-road on The Curragh things could get interesting I'm not going to tell him what doesn't kill you makes you stronger he already knows what doesn't kill you just kills you slower

Word Salad

When making lengthy explanations or reading continuously, they (the patients) drop into a meaningless extravagant jabber which Forel most happily designates as "wordsalad" (wortsalat)
– The Medical Standard 1895

His words are shredded purple cabbage
      punctuated with phrases of radicchio
subordinate to roasted butternut squash
      and Kalamata olives
His sentences are salty feta cheese
      confabulated by croutons
structured like grated carrot and cucumber
      undermined by garden rocket
His paragraphs are chopped bell peppers
      sprinkled with almonds
manifested as pumpkin seeds in disguise
      styled by red onions
His questions are tossed in vinaigrette dressing
      composed of olive oil
balsamic vinegar and Dijon mustard
      associated with sunflower seeds
His tears are commas and exclamation marks
      drizzled with a lemon reduction
mixed with a twist of pink Himalayan rock salt
      they fall like Manuka honey

Ward Warning

On the war
d are two kin
ds of people – the list
eners and the deaf. The deaf
talk to each other using eye
language. They write in cod
e in or
ange files like crayfish.
They we
ar bad
ges with names the names are mad
e up like Ma
ry O'Flaherty.
The
y hand out sweets in fair
y cups they call us pat
ients but go
d told me they a
re spi
ders. The list
eners stick to the wa
lls they wear head-phones
to he
ar me
ssages from war
zones and so
ngs and words so
they know the res
cuers a
re coming.

Mental Health Act

Section 1

Rise early, without complaint. Shower, shave,
dress in clean, pressed clothes – slovenliness
will be noted. Pre-empt admonishments
by making bed as if for a visitor,
sheet corners folded and tucked,
pillows plumped, duvet shaken
crease-free. No cuddly toys.

Section 2

Accept medications with good humour to avoid
under-tongue inspections. Attend meetings,
consultations, group work, therapy.
Engage voluntarily in recreation –
chess, card games. Follow rules.
Mention mindfulness at every
opportunity. Lower voice.

Section 3

Clear personal space of religious icons, replace
with photos of dogs/cats. Posters of idols
attract suspicion, form-filling. Prepare
list of small-talk topics – sport, food,
weather, gardening all acceptable,
steer clear of memories, truth-
telling, comedy.

Section 4

Staring into space highly dangerous. Carry
notebook, write plans for future, state
goals in manageable steps. No rants,
manifestos, revenge plots, poetry.
Put name forward for recovery
programmes, self-help
support sessions.

Section 5

Offers of assistance to cleaners, new recruits
will be regarded favourably. Non-
compliance fatal. Resistance
futile. Escape punishable
by seclusion. Listen, nod,
no questions. Beware
revolving doors.

Eyewitness

At five-to they start getting antsy
         drop smoke butts
   into almost empty pop bottles
      wet sugar turns paper and ash to mush.

At one, the wounded birds flock to the dining room
        (fattening is mandatory)
   but some stay scrawny they pick and sip and hide bread
            under shirt cuffs
scratch bald patches where feathers used to grow
before the falls from electricity wires and collisions with windowpanes.

At quarter-past they shimmy-shammy along polished corridors
    to their dormitories peel mismatched socks off their claws
    retrieve fivers
      let blisters breathe.

At two, they sing and whistle out of tune
    compare wing clippings
       did you bring tobacco?
         they sing and whistle out of tune
did you bring tobacco?

At three, a man throws a green tennis ball outside on the lawn
   for his golden retriever   the birds sit on the windowsills
     and stare
        eyes wide and dry
they have forgotten how to blink.

At half-past, they flap around my car
    leave their mark on the hood and roof
        Yeah, I'll be back tomorrow
            Sure, I'll bring tobacco
No, I won't forget.

The One Where You Look at an Ancient Painting and See Your Son

after "Achilles reaches for the shadow of Patroclus" 1803, Henry Fuseli – (Homer, Iliad XXIII, 99–110)

No one could understand Achilles, throwing himself in the dirt like a child as if Patroclus dying in battle was world-ending. Witnesses claimed that he wailed and clung to the body for hours until sleep took him. Patroclus appeared, as vision or spirit and giving out yards he was, furious, rambling, saying the funeral arrangements upset him. Typical Achilles, reached for his right-hand man's arm only to touch nothing but air. Inconsolable, refused all sustenance; porridge of barley-meal, lamb in wine marinade, salted fish, octopus, cucumber, apricots. *Patroclus' phrenes were missing* he repeated ad nauseum. State of him. Thetis, his Mammy, rose up from the sea to console her son, promised to buy him new armour. Puts me in mind of my firstborn son, seven years battling, unarmed and unarmoured, waiting for dawn to break.

Fabric
after Anne Carson

'His mother saw it mothers are like that' –

they work with invisible thread
sewing cloth or lace so that mendings
blend into the weave

long after danger has passed
you refuse red meat
dine only on white:
bread, pasta, vanilla ice-cream

your brother's head xylophoning the bannisters
the ambulance
and the black maria
waiting

Let me fetch my needle
slip stitch your thoughts
hold them in place
with this unbreakable thread

almost good as new

On the Occasion of Learning That He is Missing

You will find out it is a myth that you must wait twenty-four hours to report to the police.

You will be judged for not having a recent physical photo of him in your possession at 3am.

Your breathing will sound like a broken exhaust pipe on a clapped-out Mini Cooper whether you are a smoker or not.

Smoking will be your lifeline.

Food will repulse you and yet you may have a craving for Angel Delight or Smash potato.

Contrary to storylines on TV/film you will not take to the drink.

Your washing machine and/or fridge freezer will break down.

Sleep will become an unnecessary state.

The police will ask if you have tried phoning him.

You will not be sedated.

If your son was last seen wearing a track suit/certain brand trainers both he and you will be judged.

You will not waste your time sniffing his clothing/crying into his pillow/clutching cuddly toys in his childhood bedroom.

The price of petrol will not be a consideration when you drive around looking for him.

While searching you will see him everywhere. It will not be him.

Contrary to storylines on TV/film the police will not trace his phone.

A solicitor you do not know will phone to say your son has been in court for committing a crime he did not know he was committing.

The police who arrested him for the crime will say they did not know he was missing.

The judge will judge the police for bringing to court a person who needs medical attention and will instruct the police to bring him to hospital.

The hospital will phone to say they will not admit him because he will say there is nothing wrong with him.

He will also say the police are in league with you and the government to have him locked up.

He will also say you are not his real mother/father.

You will feel like you are living in a dystopian nightmare.

You will be living in a dystopian nightmare.

The hospital will allow him to leave before you get there. He will be wearing shorts, a t-shirt, no shoes.

It will be December.

Ballast

I do not sleep
while I wait for the phone to ring
time is a body in a flotation chamber
I am neither sound nor solid.
A stranger will tell me
he is either dead or found
I have rehearsed both in my mind
during six weeks
of fluid dread.

I walk   I stand   I sit
but can't feel my feet
they have swollen to twice their usual size
as if all my unshed tears have pooled there
like ballast in a ship's hold
keeps the vessel balanced
so it doesn't capsize in high seas.

There is an echo on the line
my own words mock me
Where is he?
Where is he?

After the call
I lie on my bed
legs raised against the wall
stay there till my ankles reappear
& time turns on the light
dries salt water
off its skin.

Black Coat

I could say that the words *gone missing* are far too close to *gone fishing* and the term *misper* as shorthand for *missing person* makes me throw up. What I will say is that when he disappeared the thought crossed my mind that if the worst happened, my black coat had seen better days, was certainly unfit for a son's funeral and replacing it right then was out of the question in case I'd be tempting fate and if the worst actually happened it would not be the time to go shopping so the coat would have to do and it really didn't matter one way or the other so why was I even worried about it? Then he was found and I forgot all about the black coat because I didn't need it and have not needed it since and maybe will never need it and please God he will be the one in need of a black coat for my final disappearance and I will make sure he has one ready so he won't have to think about it and a black coat will be the last thing on his mind and he can say something poetic to describe my disappearance and he can talk about the day we went shopping for his black coat and it won't be morbid at all, it might even be amusing and it will be a fine black coat with plenty of wear in it.

The Blues

The men in white coats don't wear white coats any more
    they wear grey sports jackets and open-necked shirts
        expensive ones
            in unthreatening colours
                duck-egg blue   champagne pink   cornsilk yellow

Sometimes the men not in white coats are women
    who wear dresses covered in fleur-de-lis patterns
        or tea-green tops
            with navy culottes
                and genuine leather tan Chelsea ankle boots

Their nails are French-polished and their hair is bobbed
    neither short nor long but cut just below the chin
        sprayed in position
            no ribbons   no scrunchies
                trimmed every six weeks   tell-tale roots covered

None of the men or women wear jewellery except for a wedding band
    unlike their clients who wear rings on all fingers including thumbs
        they have ear   nose   tongue
            and belly-button piercings
                tens of chains around their throats and wrists

All must be relinquished on admittance   a single sleeper earring
    could be fatal   strings are cut from tracksuit bottoms
        laces ripped from Docs
            belts unleashed from jeans
                so the incompetent become experts in knot-tying
And running barefoot.

Coffee Sonnet

We sat in Butler's Café   removed from
the silence of home   escaped from the ward
noise   nurses orders   mandated meal-times.
The barista made you a latte heart
raised a shy smile   my Americano
hot on my lips   my words took baby steps
across two metres of space   I wonder though
are we even half-way there yet   seven years in
no end in sight. We shared salt caramels
truffles   hazelnut brownies   every dark
mouthful drew you out   drew me in   our tongues
ungoverned. Over the hiss of the milk frother
we talked and listened like strangers
your leg shaking my hands shredding napkins.

Marks and Sparks

        The supermarket is a wonderful place
                        to be on this Wednesday
my parallel parking
          a one-handed triumph
                  for a change
     you don't forget to retrieve
                   a plastic bag from the boot
           grab a basket
                  hold your meal plan in your head

     You choose asparagus spears
                  new baby potatoes cherry tomatoes
substitute sea trout for sold-out cod
                          without a word
        check use-by dates
              and marked-down prices
      remember olive oil
              pancakes for tomorrow's breakfast

     The self-service till does not faze you
                  neither does the card payment machine
or the automated voice
        or the flickering lights
                  or the manager's eyes
You weigh and press and pack and enter your pin number
                          as if it's nothing
I walk behind you to the car
              your back and shoulders broader now
                     preparing for the day
      when you will carry your burdens alone

You load up the boot then spark a celebratory cigarette

We done well today Mum
                                                   I take the long way back
      drop you and your bags at the front door

to your new home

watch you waving in my rearview

                              as the electric gates open

Legacy
after Mary Oliver

If you must know
    I've not done much
        with my one wild and precious life

I don't know anything
    about the life cycle of gnats
        or how grass grows

I've not been an activist
    agitator   outspoken spokesperson
        leader or influencer

I have wasted my talents
    didn't know I had any
        until it was almost too late

I have slept with all
    the wrong people
        stayed in all the wrong jobs

I have no retirement plan
    or any plan
        financial or otherwise

All I have to show
    for my decades on this earth
        is the ability to speak one language

And three children
>	who have inherited
>>		my lack of interest in gardening

I have one skill learned thirty-three years ago
>	which is non-transferable
>>		to most situations:

the capacity to listen
>	and tell the difference between a baby's
>>		cry of tiredness from one of hunger

Today I taught my son
>	how to tie his hair up
>>		into a man-bun

Something to remember me by

Acknowledgements

'Admissions' 'Word Salad' and 'Coffee Sonnet' were shortlisted in the Manchester Writing Prize 2020
'Hyperemesis Gravidarum' was published in *Erbacce Journal*.
'The Wayfarer' was published in the anthology *Horses of a Different Colour* (Dempsey & Windle)
'Uninvited Guest' won 2nd prize in the Slipstream Poetry Competition 2021
'Ward Warning' won 1st prize in the iYeats International Poetry Competition 2015
'Mental Health Act' won 3rd prize in the Wolverhampton Literary Festival Poetry Competition 2018
'Eyewitness' was published in *Abridged*
'The One Where You Look at an Ancient Painting and See Your Son' was published in *Belfield Literary Review*
'Ballast' was shortlisted in the Wildfire Words/Frosted Fire Poetry Contest 2023
'The Blues' was published in the *Same Page* anthology (University College Cork)
My gratitude to The Arts Council of Ireland for an Agility Award and DLR Arts Office for Emerging Artist and Professional Development Grants which assisted me in the completion of this manuscript.
Thanks to members of the Late Night Diners and Wednesday Words poetry groups for their encouragement and eagle-eyed feedback.
Special thanks to Dr. Casey Jarrin, mentor, friend, poet.
Thanks to Jane Clarke, judge of the Poetry Business International Book & Poetry Competition for selecting this pamphlet and to Ann and Peter Sansom for editing and publishing it.
To my family, thanks for everything.